TED Books

The Hot Young Widows Club

Lessons on Survival from the Front Lines of Grief

NORA McINERNY

TED Books
Simon & Schuster
New York London Toronto Sydney New Delhi

Interior design by MGMT. design
Jacket design by MGMT. design

Manufactured in the United States of America

10 9 8 7 6 5 4 3 2 1

Library of Congress Cataloging-in-Publication Data is available.

ISBN 978-1-9821-0998-1
ISBN 978-1-9821-0999-8 (ebook)

For Moe, and all my Hot Young Widows

CONTENTS

The Hot Young
Widows Club

What this book is not:

- A collection of bummer stories.
- A definitive guide to sadness.
- A competition between you and me and everyone else to see who has the Saddest, Worst, Most Tragic Story of All Time.

That last one is important.

If we all took our personal tragedies and lined them up for comparison, we would find that someone always has it worse, and someone always has it better than us. We'd quickly find ourselves ranking our losses against one another, deciding who deserves more sympathy, more compassion. I've heard a million times that comparison is the thief of joy. But it's the thief of grief, too. And of empathy. Comparison is a dirty scoundrel who will snatch anything you leave hanging out of your pocket, so protect yourself with one of those little travel wallets that tucks up under your shirt and requires you to partially disrobe in order to pay for your lunch. OR, we can all just agree to suspend our reflex to compare, at least for the coming pages. Deal? Deal.

In my regular life, I host a podcast where I talk about people's hardest life experiences. I've spoken with rape survivors, people dying of cancer, people who have lost their hands and feet, people whose entire families have died. And I've gotten thousands of emails from people who have survived or are currently *trying* to survive the death of their children, the trauma of abuse, or the loneliness and heartbreak of infertility.

When people reach out to me to share their stories, they often say, "Now, this doesn't compare to . . ." As a preemptive strike against my judgment, or the judgment of others, they take the biggest thing that has happened in their life and shrink its significance.

Why?

What does the size of someone else's loss have to do with the size of my own? What is this macabre contest, and who could possibly win?

At thirty-one, I was a widowed mother of one. I'd just lost a parent (RIP, Dad), a husband (RIP, Aaron), and a pregnancy (RIP, Baby Deuce).

As many internet commenters have reminded me, there is nothing special about what happened to me, or what happened to Aaron. They are right, because people die all day, every day. And they are wrong, because it is all very special. Because it is ours, and it happened just to us.

I am the only woman who lost Aaron as a husband (I hope). And you are the only person who went through exactly what you went through, exactly how you went through it.

I will confess right now that I do not *love* when people compare them losing their pet bird to me losing my husband, but then . . . I've never lost a bird.

There is no conversion chart that would help us quantify and weigh these losses, no yardstick we can use to measure them against one another.

Maybe you haven't gone through *anything* hard yet. Maybe everyone you love is still alive, and the most difficult part of your life so far has been your middle school awkward phase. Well, just wait. You'll go through something eventually. A whole lot of somethings, actually. And what you have gone through, or will go through, doesn't compare to what I've gone through, and never will. The good news is, it doesn't need to.

Grief is just one of the hard things you'll experience in your life. Not just once, either. You'll get multiple servings, even when you raise your hands and say, "Really. That's enough now. I'd like to try the Joy if it's still available." At this point in the book, it's probably easy to see why I have such a busy social life. Who *wouldn't* want to spend their time with a woman who is constantly reminding you that everyone you love will die and that each death will bring a fresh new brand of grief?

Grief has the ability to maroon us on our own little island of emotion. The rest of the world is pretending it's still Tuesday, but you know the truth: that time has stopped completely, that ice cream will never taste good again, that you will never not feel the abyss inside your chest. Comparing our grief against some unknowable Grief Yardstick has the strangest effect. It takes the universality of grief and makes it so special, so unique, that our islands get smaller and more remote.

It's tempting, isn't it? To hold our losses up to the light like some kind of jeweler would, looking at all the things that make them so very unique? I knew for a fact that when Aaron died I didn't need anybody to help me through it. I scoffed at grief support groups. I bet you've never truly scoffed before—it's terribly pretentious—but I actually did. I *scoffed*. I said aloud, "What are they going to tell me that I don't already know?" What they would have told me were their own stories. They would have told me my own story. The circumstances, the names, the details, those would be different for every person in the circle of folding chairs in the hospital conference room. But the feeling—that unsoothable ache—would be the same in all of us.

They would have told me what I would like to tell you: that grief grants you admission to a club you had no intention of joining. You're admitted whether the loss is yours—*your* husband, *your* sister—or whether the loss is more tangential. Grief is a rock thrown into a still pond—even the smallest pebble ripples outward.

This book is a club of its own. Not just for those who have survived the death of a spouse, but for anyone who has loved someone who died, or who has loved someone who loved someone who died. It's for anyone who currently loves someone who will die, or who knows a person who loves someone who will die. For those whose grief is a hot fire burning through their lives, and those whose grief is a pile of ashes, embers glowing calmly. Some of the thoughts within are targeted to the griever, and some are targeted to the people trying to support the griever. Read it all. Because you'll need it all. Eventually, the supporter is a griever. Someday, the griever becomes a supporter. Sometimes, you'll be in both spots simultaneously, which is beyond rude and deeply unfair.

Today, you are here. And so am I.

•   •   •

My Tragedy Résumé reads as such:

Nora McInerny

Cancer Wife: 2011–2014
Chauffeur, personal chef, unlicensed nurse, and loving wife to Aaron Joseph Purmort.

Co-Founder, Hot Young Widows Club: 2014–Present
First husband, Aaron, died of brain cancer on November 25, 2014.

Dead Dads Club: 2014–Present
Dad died six weeks before Aaron. Rude!

Miscarriage Club: 2014–Present
Lost my second pregnancy a week before my dad. Beyond rude!

Prior to 2014, you will notice an absence of any tragedy whatsoever. That's because I had none. I had heard about a lot of sad things, of course, but none of them were mine. I lived a very easy, very comfortable life. I grew up as a white woman in the Midwest, daughter to two loving parents, and sister to three mostly well-adjusted siblings. I have not endured war, famine, racism, or poverty. I had some important people die, one right after another. This résumé seems like nothing at all to many people, and like a list of nightmares to other people.

I have never suffered the illusion that I am a special person. Maybe it is because I am one of four children, or maybe it is because I am painfully self-aware. One of my first thoughts after sitting with Aaron's dead body was: *Other people in the world are feeling this exact same thing, right now.*

I was very right.

There are a few things that we all have in common, no matter where we come from or what we do for a living. We are all born, we all die. And in between, we all suffer. In big ways and small ways. In ways that are as personal as they are universal.

Tragedy comes for all of us eventually, and when the hard stuff came for me, I was totally unprepared. And so was everyone in my life. In the year after Aaron died, I did all the things I was supposed to do and many I was not supposed to do. I went to therapy. I did yoga. I journaled. I screamed into a pillow. I drank a lot. I gave money to people who shouldn't have asked me for it. None of it helped as much as I wished it would. The most healing balm for my broken world was in my phone; the thing that helped me feel better wasn't feeling bad for myself but feeling with other people. I got a lot of messages from a lot of people around the world. They didn't all have dead husbands and dead dads, they all just had a really hard story that the people in their lives had stopped asking about, or maybe had never asked about. They just wanted to feel seen and heard. To be a little less lonely, even if they were just emailing a stranger on the internet.

I resisted joining any kind of support group when Aaron died. The entire idea conjured up notions of uncomfortable chairs arranged in a circle, weak coffee, and communal weeping, the kind that takes place in a church basement with terrible lighting.

And then I met Moe.

Moe and I met because we lived a few miles from each other and frequented the same coffee shop, a place whose owners were dead set on us creating a friendship. Moe's husband had died by suicide just a few months before Aaron had died of cancer. I knew her story, but I didn't know her, and my first reaction was *no thanks!* I didn't want to be a widow, and I didn't want widow friends. I just wanted to be me, without any label. The thing is, our coffee shop ladies are persuasive, and eventually I agreed to meet Moe. Our first date together was like my first date with Aaron: maybe it wasn't love at first sight, but it was obvious that I had met someone who was going to be a pillar in my life. In Moe, I found a person who knew exactly what I meant when I shared my weirdest, darkest thoughts. A person who spoke the language I was just learning.

I hadn't counted on making a friend, let alone a support group, but that's what happened. Eventually.

Moe and I called ourselves the Hot Young Widows Club. Sure, it was just two of us at first, but people with dead husbands tend to attract other people with dead husbands, and soon we had an actual group of people. Some among us were never legally married, some were divorced when our partner died. Some of us have remarried, and some of us never will. Some of us are deeply religious, and just as many of us are not. It doesn't matter. It's just a *name*, so there is no clubhouse and no criteria for joining other than the death of your partner. You don't have to be married, you don't have to be young, and your hotness is innate and inarguable to me. If the person you were spending your life with dies? You're in the club.

When we meet up in real life, there is no church basement and no coffee (unless it's brunch). There is no leader, no bylaws, no ritual. There are hugs and screams of joy; there are plenty of tears. The only thing we promise to one another is to give each other what our friends and family outside the group have such a hard time giving us: a space to just . . . be. A space where we do not need to have a plan or stay strong. A place where we do not tell each other that it will be okay, or that everything happens for a reason.

The club that started out as Moe and me, meeting for coffee and crying in public, quickly grew into a network of friends and strangers around the world who shared this particular kind of loss.

Other people wanted in, too. Could they join the club if their sister's husband had died? If their mother had been widowed? If they had lost a very close friend? The desire to belong to a group that understood loss—that welcomed the uncomfortable conversations that follow death—was astonishing. And it shouldn't have been. Because the people who *wanted* into the club were people who had noticed how woefully unprepared they had been for a woeful situation. They recognized that to create a good support system for a grieving person, they would need to know something about grief.

The *actual* Hot Young Widows Club is a series of Facebook groups. Secret ones, the kind you can't find through searching, and whose members aren't listed publicly. These digital groups of total strangers—many of whom have only their catastrophic losses in common—have a real-life impact. One of our "wids," as we say—because even sad people need a quippy nickname—is a handyman who signs in every Monday to show us how to fix things around our houses. Wids have helped one another move into new houses, get their finances in order, and create better dating profiles. Wids have vacationed together and flown into new cities just to meet up with a group of strangers who know more about their inner lives than most of their family members. Wids have gotten into commenting arguments over small things that don't really matter because, look, the internet brings out the best *and* the worst in us, and let's not even pretend we haven't all done the same thing.

The Hot Young Widows Club has taught me everything I know about survival and love and what that annoying buzzword *resilience* really means. It's a club I hope you never join. A club that is not worth the price of admission. And a club whose doors I am cracking open—just a smidge—for you. Because there are some truths that are evident regardless of what your Tragedy Résumé is or isn't: that we are all doing our best, that our best is hardly ever good enough, and that not everything is going to be okay. I cannot imagine any doctor writing a prescription for sad stories, but I wish they would. I wish that all of us would take the time to sit with the sadness of another person. To not rush through to a resolution or try to hand them a tissue or a lemon juicer. To just . . . let the sadness sit there. To feel with them.

The hard things I avoided for so long are now my job to talk about. I write about sad stuff, I talk about it on a podcast. And talking about sad things doesn't make me sad. It makes me grounded and grateful. We need the sad stories of other people because, someday, we'll be the protagonist of our own sad story, and the suffering we've witnessed will lead us through our own darkness.

Grief is a form of emotional alchemy. The loss of our closest people changes us. But we're still . . . us. Grief has no timeline, no expiration date. And sad is not all you'll ever be.

I am not a scientist, or a journalist, or a genius. I am a person who has been through some things, and so are you.

If you've ever suffered or struggled, if you've had a grenade of loss blast your whole world open or watched helplessly while someone else's life was blown apart, you're not alone. Or you may not have had your tragedy . . . yet. Whatever your Tragedy Résumé reads, welcome to the club.

1 Am I Grieving Right?

A common idea of grief is that it will include a lot of crying, and a lot of Kleenex. Yes, for some people it will. And for others, it will include a complete departure from their typical personality or behaviors. When you experience a foundational loss, your world is so shaken that you become accustomed to turbulence. It seems almost safer to keep the plane bouncing along, to create your own dips and turns.

Every grieving person I know experienced their own brand of self-inflicted turbulence. They each had their own weird grief activities that you don't see printed in typical grief books. One woman I know spent eight hundred dollars on pots and pans after her husband died. I was not aware that it was possible to spend eight hundred dollars on pots and pans, but I *was* aware that it's possible to spend eight hundred dollars on workout clothes, which is something I did.

I spent a *lot* of money after Aaron died. This is different from having a lot of money to spend, and having recently quit my job, I did not have a lot of money. But I had a huge, gaping hole in the center of my soul and it felt like I could fill it with things if I tried hard enough. I gave it a solid effort, but the hole remained.

Not everyone spends money like crazy after they lose someone they love. But a lot of us do! A lot of us start drinking more than we did before. And a lot of us get tattoos. Or sleep around. We're not breaking any rules, except the one that nobody knows the origin for, the one that says grief always equals sadness.

Grief is sadness, but it's also an unscratchable itch, an insatiable hunger, an unsoothable ache. It is an extreme discomfort that's both spiritual and physical. After Aaron's death, I could feel my heart beating harder and faster in my chest. The muscles in my shoulders, neck, and head tightened into thick knots. My head ached constantly.

"I just want to take out my eyes and massage them gently," I said to a widow friend.

"I know exactly what you mean!" she said, and we sat on my couch, pressing the heels of our hands against our eyes in silence for a few minutes before unloading our anxieties on each other.

I was worried about money at the time. Probably because I was bleeding money through late-night Amazon purchases and was constantly in danger of overdrawing my checking account. She was worried about her reputation. She'd met a man online and had slept with him after their second date. She hadn't liked him that much, but she'd liked the idea of him, and the feeling of him. She'd had wild, uninhibited sex with a guy she barely knew, and it was awesome. It was awesome because she got to be radically in the moment, and in her body. That sex was a respite from the grief that had consumed her.

And while she wasn't interested in that guy anymore, she was definitely interested in having more sex with someone else. Was that excessive? Was it okay? Nobody could tell how much money I spent, but someone could, conceivably, run into her out and about on a date in our city. What would they think?

If you haven't been widowed before, you may be thinking, *Oh yuck, what a maladaptive coping mechanism!*

It's very easy to judge where someone is when you haven't been there.

And it's easy to justify every purchase and every decision when you are sad. I said out loud many times, "My husband is dead! I can do what I want!" It became a catchphrase for me and Moe, my Hot Young Widows Club co-founder. We could do whatever we wanted! We could get more tattoos. I could change my hair color from lavender to blond to a blue that turned green accidentally. I could quit my job! I could start a nonprofit and write a book! I could move in with my mom if I wanted to! What looked spontaneous or even bizarre to the people around me made perfect sense to me. My dad and my husband and my last baby with Aaron were dead. So what if I lose some money, or some hair? So what if I get a bad tattoo?

My in-box is filled with people who are mystified by their grief behaviors. They are wondering if they are normal. They want to know if they are grieving right.

Why would a suburban mother suddenly want a neck tattoo? How could a person who just watched his wife die of cancer have an appetite for sex? Why do they always feel like they have the flu?

I tell them all the same thing, which is that I am not a doctor or a licensed therapist, but I *am* an enthusiastic, amateur grief anthropologist. Which is my way of saying that I've seen a lot of people grieve a lot of different ways and I consider them all normal.

It is normal to hate your friend because their husband is alive and yours is not. It is normal to bristle at seemingly innocuous questions like, "How are you holding up?" It is normal to catalog all the mistakes your friends and family are making around you and your grief. It's normal to not shed a tear at your child's funeral, but then to sob uncontrollably in the Target parking lot when you see their doppelgänger toddling through the automatic doors. It's all terrible, and uncomfortable, and miserable, and normal.

An Incomplete List of Grief Things That Are Normal

- Giving all your husband's clothes away the day after he dies

- Asking for his clothes back several months later

- Hating your aunt because she was noisily making a sandwich in the kitchen while your grandmother was dying in her hospital bed just yards away; also hating HGTV and the Property Brothers for making "open concept" houses so ubiquitous

- Fighting over the wording of an obituary

- Balking at the cost of the funeral lunch and deciding people can just have some light snacks instead

- Wearing your dead husband's socks

- Seeing your dead person in every crowd, and momentarily forgetting that they are dead

- Keeping anything the dead person may have touched

- Selling or donating everything the dead person may have touched

- Staying in your house
- Leaving your house
- Spreading the ashes in a solemn ceremony
- Keeping the ashes in your closet for five years, then finally dumping them in the backyard
- Not sending thank-you cards for all the nice things people did, because the idea of sitting down to write a thank-you card when the person you love so much is *dead* just seems absolutely ridiculous
- Celebrating your dead person's birthday
- Celebrating your dead person's deathday (I prefer to say deathaversary)
- Feeling like you will never love again
- Feeling like you could, and possibly did, fall in love with a body pillow
- Getting very into fitness
- Getting very into drinking (not advised)
- Getting very into staring at your phone for twelve hours a day

2 I Feel Like I'm Losing My Mind

You are absolutely losing it right now. You can't remember where you put your keys, you can't recall where you parked the car. You can't remember why you picked up your phone, or what you were going to say. You can't remember the word for . . . anything. You forget where you said you'd be, and when. You're double booked. Triple booked. You're canceling everything to stay home and stay in bed.

My widows call it Widow Brain, but other people call it Grief Fog or Grief Brain or OH MY GOD WHAT IS HAPPENING TO ME?!

I was sure I had early onset Alzheimer's. Just before my husband died, I told my husband's neurologist that it felt like my brain was a wet sponge that couldn't take in any other information. He nodded. "Makes sense," he said. He was a man of few words, but he explained to me that I did have a lot going on. A lot of traumatic things. You know, like watching my husband die for three years, and then having my dad beat him to the punch after only having cancer for five minutes.[*] My brain was just . . . full, like a very old computer. I'd need to just wait for it to

---

[*] More like five months but, like I said, I was losing my mind.

reboot. Turn it off and then on again. Whatever it is you do with computers when they're not working.

My Widow Brain got worse after I became an actual widow. I'd put the milk in the cabinet and the cereal in the fridge. I couldn't read more than a few sentences at a time. I had a hard time remembering which day of the week it was, and a typical conversation with me went something like this:

Me: I just need to . . . you know . . . I was going to, uh . . . like I said, as soon as we . . . What were we talking about?

You: *blinks and shrugs*

Grief changes us. And while we mostly like to talk about the ways it *improved* us, how it gave us perspective and a new lease on life, how it has made our lives richer and more meaningful . . . not all change is easy, or for the best. Widow Brain is an invisible illness that makes you feel batty and incapable when you're already vulnerable. I've found it to be like a fog that rolls in and out, typically settling in around Aaron's deathaversary. It's not as heavy as it once was, but it reminds me of how disorienting and dark it can be to lose someone you love.

If the old you was not just on the ball, but on the ball while wearing heels and juggling flaming torches, and this new you is getting hit with the ball . . . get a helmet, because this is what your life is going to be like for a while. You aren't who you used to be, and you won't always be this person, either. You won't always be looking for your keys in the bottom of your trash can before realizing you actually threw them in the recycling bin.

It's been four years since Aaron died, and I still use a combination of tactics to keep my mind and life running as smoothly as possible. I meditate, I eat right, and I get nine hours of sleep a night.

I'm kidding, those are the kind of aspirational self-care things that I'd like to say helped me, but what really got me through the fog was Post-it notes, to-do lists, and my calendar app.

I assume at all times that my brain is still a wet sponge, and anything you tell me will just run right off me. But I don't have a life where I can just shrug off all my responsibilities and tell everyone, *"Sorry! I forgot."* I now have four kids, and they really dislike when I forget to pick them up from things, or when their concerts start, or where their soccer practice is. Likewise, my friends don't love it when I forget their birthday parties, or when I forget to invite them to my wedding (sorry, Hannah!).

If you feel like you're losing your mind in the wake of your grief . . . you are.

•   •   •

A Guide to Grief Brain

Write everything down. Everything. There is no such thing as *"Oh, I'll remember that"* anymore. Your brain can no longer be trusted with your schedule, your ideas, or your to-do lists. I keep stacks of Post-it notes around my house so when I have a realization, I can jot it down immediately. If I'm lying in bed, just about to fall into a deep, luxurious sleep, and I remember there is something I *must* do the next day, I don't chance it. I sit up, grab a pen and a Post-it from my bedside table, and write it down.

Gather it up. You can't live in a house that is wallpapered in sticky notes, so you need to remember to take all these Post-its and condense the information. I'm sure you have five to-do list apps on your phone right now, but none of them will feel as satisfying as writing everything down in list form and crossing them out when you're done. I don't know if I believe in heaven, but if I do, it has to be the feeling you get when you complete a to-do.

Calendar it. Your magical computer phone has one very important app: the calendar. Every part of my day is on my calendar. My gym schedule, our family's dinner plans, even who is picking which kid up from what. It's all on the calendar. On weekends, I go over the calendar and my to-do lists to make sure I'm not missing anything. I used to feel self-conscious asking people to send me calendar invites for things like *Having lunch with our friends!* But by now, anyone who knows me well enough to eat a meal with me should also know that if it's not on my calendar, it's not happening.

Expect less. I am a part of a business-lady group that meets once a month to make sure our businesses are on track and we're meeting our goals. At one meeting, one of our group members was walking us through her business performance for the previous year. She was 20 percent down on revenue, she explained. Possibly because her brother died? I let her finish the rest of her presentation, and then shot my hand up. Did she just say her revenue was down 20 percent because her brother had died? She nodded. This woman had just experienced an

elemental loss—a sibling!—and didn't see how astonishing it was
that she hit 80 percent of her revenue goal even though she'd
spent most of the year watching her brother fade from this earth.
We would never expect another person to maintain perfection in
the face of grief, but we sure expect it from ourselves, like grief is
something that can be managed like the many calendar systems
I have been telling you to implement. It isn't. And you need the
calendars and the Post-its and the to-do lists because you are not a
machine, and grief is not a program you can run. You are a person.
Your house may not be perfectly clean anymore. You may not
hit your revenue goal. Your kids might start eating Happy Meals
twice a week. So what? If there was ever a time to lower the bar
for yourself, this is it. Grade yourself on the grief curve, where 80
percent isn't a B–, it's a gosh dang A++.

Eyes on your own paper. Did you know that so-and-so is doing *so
well* after their child died? Doesn't whatsherface look better than
ever? You'd never guess that just a year ago, her entire life fell apart!
All around you there are people who appear to be doing so much
better than you are with your grief. Maybe they are, and maybe they
just spend all night screaming into a pillow, and then post self-helpy
things on Instagram. A widow I know recently said, "I thought
I'd be doing better than this. It's been three years." As if her grief
had long expired. Why did she think she should be doing better?
Because it seemed like a lot of other widows were doing better than
she was. Beyond comparing our grief, we tend to compare the way
we're dealing with grief. Her grief is hers. Your grief is yours. You
have a responsibility to do it your way, in your own time.

3 Something Terrible Just Happened

If Aaron had died a hundred years ago, I'd have taken my cue from Queen Victoria and dressed in black for an entire year. I may even have donned a widow's cap—a very fetching and dramatic headpiece that would surely make an impression at day-care pickup. I would have had a uniform that would signal to other people that I had experienced a monumental loss and should be treated with care, and possibly avoided on the sidewalk. But Aaron died in 2014, and I was not a queen. I was a widowed mom in the American Midwest. I had bills to pay and a little mouth to feed and a huge sea of grief to try and swim through with both hands tied behind my back.

I did not know how to do this.

And neither did anyone around me. If you can believe it, when my husband died at age thirty-five, he was the first of his friends to die. Nobody else in our immediate circle had been a caregiver for their husband yet. Nobody else had realized the importance of a health-care directive.

The immediate aftermath of a death keeps a grieving mind and heart busy and numb. A funeral is a lot of planning, and that to-do list gives you the illusion that you know what you're doing, that grief is just a series of boxes to tick through. A to-do list is clear and contained and easy for anyone to pitch in on. It's a perfect blueprint for how to be supportive in the face of loss. My mother called a caterer for the funeral, my sister arranged for the space, Aaron's childhood friend made his urn. Even beyond our inner circle, the compartmentalization and commoditization Americans have done with grief meant that everyone around us knew what to do next. No matter how confounding or devastating a death, there are a few easy steps that anyone can handle:

1. Send a card
Preferably something in soft colors, with vaguely reassuring and nondenominational wording. Make sure it doesn't say *dead* or *death* anywhere on it. It should offer your sympathies, or, even better, your condolences. I like condolences because it sounds like a nice, warm pastry.

2. Bring some food
Never mind that the grieving person has no appetite and that everything tastes like sand and sawdust with a dash of bitterness. Where I come from, we know that the only cure for a broken heart is a nice, warm dish of cheese and carbs, baked at 350°F for thirty minutes.

3. Go to the funeral
You don't have to stay for the macabre ham sandwich luncheon afterward, but you do have to show up and show your sad face to the bereaved. Again, offer some

condolences. Remember to wear something black, or close to black, to stand as far from the front as possible, and to sign the guestbook so they know you were there.

4. Move on with your life

Congratulations! You did it! You helped someone through their grief!

Except that once the noise and the business of a funeral is over, and the bereavement leave is done, the grief starts to wake up from its hibernation. And we don't have a to-do list for that.

Beyond those first, mindless steps, *none of us* knows what we are doing with grief, or loss, or tragedy. Anyone proclaiming to be some kind of expert is . . . not. Because every single loss is different, even if you've been through a thousand of them. You may have lost your mother and your brother, but when your father dies, it is the first and only time you will lose him. You may have a nephew with congenital heart disease, but when you encounter it in a stranger, it won't be the same. Each of these experiences is a new one for you, and for everyone around you.

Because I was the person closest to the loss, everyone in my life looked to me for guidance. What were they supposed to do or say? Where was the line between inquiry and intrusion? How long was this process going to last, anyway? I was their disoriented leader, wandering in circles through the wilderness.

A good leader would turn to look the group in the face, perhaps even get down on one knee. "Team," she'd say, looking them all in the eye, "I have no idea what I'm doing." The group would honor her vulnerability and rally around her. Together, this ragtag crew would hack their way through grief and come out stronger and closer on the other side.

But I was not a good leader. I didn't have enough vision to recognize that I was lost, or the humility to admit it. Now I see that incompetence is an opportunity. I sound like an inspirational poster with an eagle on it, but there's a reason why those posters grace every single office building in America! Because they're just simple enough to be true, no matter what.

My friend Emily McDowell, the creator of a wildly popular set of Empathy Cards, said, "Connection is about being fucked up together. There is no humanity in perfection." Perfection is not just boring, it's isolating and inhuman.

Why should we be good at something like this? Why should we automatically be A+ students at something so chaotic and messy?

I had no idea what grief was, or what it even looked like.

The closest I'd come to seeing grief was in middle school, when my uncle Tom fell from the roof of a construction project he was working on. He spent a few weeks in a coma before he died on November 3, his mother's birthday. I saw my parents cry when Tom had his accident. I saw them fall apart at his funeral. My father had cried in front of me just one other time, when my grandfather had died two years before. After Tom's funeral, we never spoke of him again. I spent my nights in bed crying quietly for him, thinking that I must be going crazy. Nobody else in my house was crying. My mother still woke up and went to work. She made our lunches and dinners and sat next to my father reading every night. Life had gone back to normal, but I had not. I assumed that I was defective. That my eyes wouldn't stop leaking and my heart wouldn't heal because I was doing something wrong. Grief, as I had seen it, ended at the funeral. Ashes to ashes. Dust to dust. Back in the station wagon and back to real life.

I now know that there is no way that my mother was okay. Her little brother had died, leaving behind three boys who would only drift further and further away from our side of the family as they were reunited with their estranged mother. She was shattered, but she was doing her best impression of a normal mother, and she was doing it for us. She just didn't want us to worry about her, or about Dad. She didn't want our pain to become her pain. While I was crying quietly in my bed, she was crying quietly in hers.

I thought for sure that the best thing I could be as a widow, and a mother, and a woman in general, was *okay*. To not be anyone else's problem. Like my mother, I did a very, very good impression of an okay person. I wore lipstick every day, I made sure that my Instagram posts weren't too sad, I filled my days with activities designed to keep me busy and keep me from feeling.

It didn't work. The grief leaked out of the cracks and out of my eyes. It kept me up all night. And I kept it all to myself.

The question I heard the most after Aaron died was the question I heard the most *before* he died:

"How are you?"

It's a question that we lob at each other casually, walking down the hallway at work, or greeting the cashier at the grocery store. It's a huge, meaningful question, but one that has been whittled down to just small talk. It's a question that we know can only be answered with a response as pithy as the spirit in which this question was asked. We *have* to say "fine" or "good," because to say "my husband died a year ago and I still feel like I've swallowed a molten rock of grief that is lodged in my solar plexus" would mean breaking the social contract that insists we put our best and happiest face forward.

So we say nothing. Or we say "fine" and "good." We nod and we smile, and we keep that molten rock of grief to ourselves.

That's the safe thing to do with our grief. It's a scary feeling, and it's even scarier to think about how the people around us could react if they knew the truth of how this felt.

●   ●   ●

I am writing this from the American Midwest, a land of notoriously thrifty people. A land of coupon clippers and deal seekers, people who will camp out in nature, or camp outside of a big box store for a Black Friday sale. Compliment any Midwesterner on their outfit and they will tell you how little they paid for it, the number of coupons they used to obtain it, and how they got an additional 10 percent off because there was a loose button that they just went home and fixed themselves! If there is a deal to be had, we will find it, use it, and brag about it forever.

This thriftiness extends to us emotionally, too, though that trait is not exclusive to Midwesterners. The cheapest and easiest emotion any of us humans can access is pity, and we are awfully generous with it. We pity the refugees whose photos we briefly see while scrolling through Facebook, we pity the person in front of us at the grocery store who doesn't have enough money to cover what she put in her cart. We pity the person standing at the freeway exit, begging for our loose change. It's easy to feel bad for someone, and I am very good at it myself. It has been a natural talent of mine from as far back as I can remember. I could and did feel bad for people all the time. Pity was a very quick way for me to feel like I was a good person, a caring person. I was affected by the suffering of others. I felt *really* bad for them, and then . . . I was done. I could check that person or that situation off my to-do list.

I was twenty-seven when my friend Gene's father died. The death was unexpected, and horrifying, and I felt really bad about it. I felt awful that my friend was sad, and that his entire family was, too. I did exactly what I knew to do: I went to the funeral. I sent a card. I may have even dropped off a hot dish (that's Midwest talk for casserole). And that was it. Gene's grief was a closed case, and there was nothing more for me to do. The entire process took a highly efficient seven days, from start to finish, but it felt like it had been ages. I never again asked Gene about his dad, because I didn't know what to say, and I didn't want to make him sad. If Gene brought up his dad's death in conversation, I changed the topic to something happier as soon as I could, like any good friend would have. In between, I often felt really, really bad that Gene's dad had died. I felt bad *for* him. I pitied Gene, and his sisters. I pitied his dead dad.

Pity didn't seem like a four-letter word until my husband died, and I was on the other end of the pity fire hose. Everywhere I went, I felt myself being showered with the pity of people around me. I couldn't stand to be around anyone. I couldn't stand to see their wet eyes, their forlorn faces, or the way they looked at my son like he was a lost puppy. It was just such a shame that Aaron had died at age thirty-five, leaving behind a wife and a child. People felt so bad for us!

I didn't want people to feel bad for me. I didn't want to see them cluck quietly to themselves when they saw my child playing on the floor during his father's funeral, or give me a sad smile in the grocery store. That pity wasn't a bridge to my pain; it was a cage around me. It made me something to look at, something to study.

"I can't imagine," people would say to me, and I would think to myself, *You have a really bad imagination.* Because I can imagine nearly anything: a dinosaur on a skateboard, a car wreck that kills my entire family, the pain that Aaron's mom felt in losing her only son. Some things are more fun to imagine than others, but the harder it is to conjure something in our minds, the more we probably need to.

Empathy is simply having a good imagination. It's feeling not from your point of view ("I don't want to go to a funeral. It's too sad. I'll feel awkward.") but from someone else's point of view ("She's just lost a child. She doesn't want to be at his funeral, either. She'd rather be picking his boogers or telling him it's time for dinner. This is harder for her than it is for me."). If this sounds like a familiar exercise, it's because our parents and grandparents and kindergarten teachers called it "walking a mile in someone else's shoes." We were too young to let the lesson sink in, probably. We just heard something about wearing someone else's shoes and thought, *Ick*.

Pity keeps our hearts closed up, locked away. Empathy opens our heart up to the possibility that the pain of others could one day be our own pain, too. Pity keeps the pain of others at arm's length. It says, "That sad thing is happening over there, but it isn't my sad thing." Pity sheds a tear and moves on. Empathy rolls up its sleeves and pitches in.

Empathy is work, and work is hard. In general, most of us do not *love* hard work. If nobody is watching us in a workout class, are we going to turn up the resistance on our stationary bikes or leave it how it is? If your office gives employees the *option* of leaving early on a Friday, you'll notice most desks are empty after lunch. In the parking lot of my local Costco, the shopping carts are just left in the middle of the parking spaces, as if the walk to the cart corral was simply *too much* for shoppers who have just loaded their cars with multiple gallons of peanut butter.

We are *all* incompetent when it comes to grief. All of us. Even (especially?) me. I have a pretty impressive list of dead people, but I still find myself searching for the right words when I'm faced with the suffering of others. Recently, I met a family at the airport who were friends of friends. We ended up in the security line together and got to talking about the only relevant topic for that line: where we were each heading. They were on their way to Boston.

"Fun!" I said while we waited in line to be frisked by the TSA.

"We're actually going to get her a lifesaving heart surgery," her mother said, and I froze.

My nephew, Gabe, has a serious and life-threatening heart defect. I know how serious it is to tinker with a kid's heart, and how nervous my sister-in-law gets just walking into a hospital with her little dude. What words of comfort did I offer this family? These ones:

"Heart surgery?? BOOO!"

I booed a little girl. And her heart surgery.

Her mother looked at me. Her father looked at me. The little girl looked at me. I had given them exactly what they feared from their admission: a big dollop of pity; a wave from the mainland. My words hung there in the air between us, lit up in neon.

"I'm such an idiot," I admitted. "I have no idea what to say."

The little girl had moved on to a more interesting topic, her iPad. Her parents, though, burst into laughter. And then I did, too.

They had the grace to realize that not everyone—even a person who talks about death and loss and grief for a living—knows what to do with a life-threatening childhood disease. And I had the humility to just call myself out. To admit that I was not the best at what we were talking about, and that I had rushed to fill a silence—and filled it with hot, flaming garbage.

I hated a lot of people for saying the wrong thing to me, and sometimes *still* do, until I remember that I once booed a little girl in an airport.

If you are grieving and feel alone, if you have found yourself distancing yourself from someone just because you don't know what to say, I have the exact words you need. You've said them before, just not to the person who needs to hear them.

It goes like this:

"I have no idea what I'm doing."

Then go and be fucked up together. Be human.

4 For the Lonely

It's not just in your head.

Grief is lonely.

Death was just the beginning, it turns out. You lost a person, and then you kept losing people. They didn't all die, although sometimes that happens, and it is a shame that the funeral directors don't offer some sort of frequent-griever discount card. People you love tend to just . . . disappear. Not literally—you still follow them on Facebook, so you know that their husband just got a promotion and they recently spent a long weekend in the Upper Peninsula of Michigan. But they call less, and then not at all. When you see them at Target, you'll both say you should get together soon. You both know that it will not be happening.

Each of us is the hub for our very own social wheel. Your person was the hub of their own social wheel. The connections and friendships and relationships that revolved around them were not all automatically transferred to you. A dynamic was forever shifted.

Six months after losing a pregnancy, my husband, and my father, the list of losses was only growing longer. The dozens of friends on my list had winnowed itself down to three. My favorite family members were now near-strangers. Not

everyone who disappeared from my life was a bad person—
they're all actually pretty good people—they are just incompetent
people. People who didn't know what they were doing, and
people I didn't have the energy to instruct. The loneliness of grief
is not just emotional. It's not just that you are suffering through
a feeling that is unique to you and your relationship. It's a real,
tangible loneliness. It's a phone that stops ringing, parties that
you're not even invited to.

The luckiest among us will maintain the exact same social
circles after a loss. Their friends and family will get even
closer, more tight-knit. Most of us will wake up a year later and
find that the friends we used to be close to are now more like
acquaintances.

What is wrong with me?! I thought. What if none of these
people ever liked me? What if they'd just tolerated me because
they loved Aaron? I was convinced that their absence spoke only
to my own defectiveness. Perhaps some of it did—are any of us at
our very best in the year after we lose our partner?—but I believe
that this churn of relationships is mostly a natural by-product of
death.

Like most of the things you've impulse-purchased on
Amazon, not every relationship is built to last for life. Some
friends are meant to last a few seasons, a decade at most. And
chasing people and convincing them you are still worthy of their
time and attention seems like a waste of the precious time you
have left on this earth.

Not every relationship will survive this death.

5 Show Up

I grew up going to a small parochial school, the kind of place where you spend nine years with the same fifty kids in your grade and grow a sort of simultaneous love and disdain for each of them. It's almost fraternal, this feeling, except that you each go home to your own siblings and parents at the end of an eight-hour day together. It was at this school that I learned the stations of the cross and the anxiety of social interaction. It was customary in our small school to extend party invitations to everyone in the grade, knowing full well that not everyone would attend. Still, an invite would go out, and you'd hope that the right people would show up. The right people were the cool kids, obviously. The ones with straight teeth and shiny hair and the ability to whip up a mob mentality wherever they went (please remember that grammar school is brutal).

That feeling—the hope for the right people to show up— stayed with me, like it probably stayed with most people who grew up on the periphery between cool and not cool. I wanted to be friends with the right people in the office, or in my industry. I wanted the right people to show up for my parties.

And I wanted the right people to show up when Aaron died. I became a meticulous scorekeeper, adept at tallying the many absences. It was easy to notice who was missing: the friends who stopped checking in, the family members who disappeared. What did I do with my exacting score? I held on to it and let each of these absences grow into a quiet grudge, a one-way resentment that created no possibility for the offender to make it up to me. I did not reach out to tell these people that I was hurt, that I had waited for them to show up and been devastated when they hadn't. Instead, I waited for *them* to come to *me*. They ought to, right? They were the ones who still had living husbands and dads and healthy second pregnancies. They should be crawling to me! Checking in via text, phone call, a random drop-by on a Saturday afternoon. They should understand my needs even without me articulating them! It was their job to be there for *me*, not the other way around. I placed myself and my suffering on a pedestal. I was superior to everyone who failed me. Beyond reproach.

At the same time I was tallying the absences of the people I expected to show up for me, I was being inundated with messages from strangers and acquaintants who wanted to know what they could do for me, how they could help me. The answer was, "I don't know." Because *I had no idea*. I had never been widowed before. I didn't know what I needed, or what I could ask of a stranger. I grew to hate that question, because it felt more like receiving a request: *"Hello, Nora, I'd like to help you. Please think of a task you're comfortable with a stranger performing, and humble yourself enough to ask me if I have the time or interest to do it."* My pride was nonexistent, so I tried my best to ask for help when I needed it. Once, I asked a close family member if she could watch Ralph for twenty minutes so I could go for a run. "I'm about to freak out," I texted. "I need to go blow off some anxiety." Her reply came an hour later. "Sorry! Have brunch plans. Another time?" I resolved to never ask anyone for anything again. If this was how a family member would reply, how would a stranger prioritize my desperation? I'd rather not find out.

I got several messages from another acquaintance who wanted to know if I'd gotten the package she'd left for me and Ralph when Aaron was dying. We got a lot of packages when Aaron was dying. I made the Executive Decision not to keep track of who sent what, and to thank who I could, when I could remember. If you really *need* a thank-you, I reasoned, then you've given me this hot dish for the wrong reason. I ran into this person several times after Aaron's death. Every single time she mentioned the package, and every single time I thanked her. *Never again!* I thought. *Never again will I accept a gift from someone I hardly know. Not if the cost is my perpetual thankfulness for something I never asked for, and probably dumped into the garbage.*

So I struggled on, doing as much as I could on my own. A few months after Aaron died, I got a message from the wife of one of Aaron's college friends. Hannah and I had somehow never met, but I knew who she was. She didn't ask how I was doing, or what she could do for me. She told me I was on her mind, and she was at Costco picking up some basics for her family. She'd grabbed some for me and Ralph, too. She'd leave it on our back step. I didn't even need to open the door. I started to protest but then I opened my fridge. The milk was gone. There were a few apples rolling around in one of the drawers. And that was it. "Thanks!" I replied. I opened the door after I saw her headlights pull out of my driveway. Ralph and I ate a real dinner that night.

Hannah and I continued on this way for some time: her offering kindness that required nothing of me, me accepting it. The night we really, truly met, I cried more with her than I had with my entire family since Aaron's death.

Here is what Hannah did that is so hard to do: she checked her ego, and in turn helped me check mine. She didn't need a thank-you. She didn't need directions. She did the things she could do, and she did them just because. No agenda. No expectation. Her gifts were transformative. Not just the Costco butter, which I now buy by the pound, but the real, true friendship. The kind where you just . . . show up.

Showing up is not just a physical act. Showing up can mean texting a person when they are on your mind or sending them a card when the cards have stopped coming and the house is quiet.

I realized later that it was easier for Hannah to show up than it was for my friends, because Hannah didn't have anything to lose. She and I didn't have any history to complicate things. She didn't know the long list of things that annoyed me, or how high my expectations were for the people I loved. She saw a hurt, she knew her own abilities, and she put the two of them together. In my own life, I have tried to be more like Hannah and less like . . . myself. I still struggle with trying to do or say the right thing when I'm faced with the suffering of others. I struggle for the same reasons you may struggle: because if you can't *fix* it, what can you do?

"What can I do?" people want to know when someone's life falls apart. And the answer to that question is a question.

"Well, what *can* you do?"

Because there's always something *you* can do. There is always a Venn diagram to be made between what you're capable of and what another person needs. Just . . . do *something*. Do it without needing a thank-you, or any acknowledgment. Do it without thinking of what makes *you* comfortable.

It is hard to be there for someone who seems like they don't need you. And I was very good at pretending I didn't need anyone. If they'd asked, I would have told them I was fine. Maybe they *did* ask—I don't remember—but if they did, I probably told them that I was okay, that there was nothing I needed for them to do. But I wanted them to see through that lie and show up anyway! To be the kind of friend or brother or aunt I didn't even know I needed! Why was it so hard for people to read my mind? And why was it so hard for me to read their minds? Because none of us are mind readers, and in moments of crisis, it's very easy for us to retreat into our minds and play an endless loop of what-ifs that prevent us from actually doing anything. The people in my life who loved me and failed me were just afraid of *doing* the wrong thing or *saying* the wrong thing, so they did nothing at all. I was afraid of the same things. That if I said just how lonely or devastated I was, just how disappointed I was, that I would burn the last bridges connecting me to the outside world.

●   ●   ●

The more complicated our relationship with the dead person, the more difficult it can be to talk about. The Hot Young Widows Club includes plenty of people who lost an ex-partner, or an estranged one. Who struggle with whether or not they have the right to be sad about someone's death, as if your feelings and history with another person are just—*poof!*—deleted from the cloud upon the dissolution of your relationship. One woman wept to me that she was the only person still grieving her ex-husband, who had died by suicide years after their divorce. She'd remarried, and he had not; and while they could not be married to each other, she still had love for him. Her new husband understood her devastation over her dead ex-husband, but her parents did not. Why was she so sad about this? They were divorced!

Now, asking someone why they're sad about their ex-husband dying by suicide seems like one of the top five stupidest questions I've ever heard, but the only person who could possibly ask that question is a person who hasn't been shaken by traumatic loss.

This woman's loneliness was palpable to me. She didn't know how to make new friends, because she wanted her friends to be the kind of people who could understand this loss. She didn't know what to say to her parents, because they were the kind of people who were flabbergasted at her sadness over the suicide of her ex-husband. She didn't know what to say to her new husband, because she thought he might feel bad about how sad she was about her ex-husband, even though he said he understood it. Even though he wanted to support her.

"Have you told your family and your husband any of this?" I asked her, and she shook her head. Her family had no idea that they'd hurt her feelings. Her husband, who had been supportive and kind to her, had no idea that she secretly feared her grief was hurting him and that he was just too nice to say anything about it.

The people who hurt you often have absolutely no idea what they've done, or how you feel. Life would be a lot simpler if we all shared an emotional Bluetooth connection that let us in on one another's innermost feelings.*

"I think you should tell them," I told her. "I think you should tell them everything you just told me, exactly how you told me."

The best-case scenario is that her family, hearing how much they've hurt their daughter, realizes their mistake and re-engages her grief with empathy. That her husband reassures her that her anxiety about his jealousy over her grief for a dead man is misplaced. The worst-case scenario is that her parents don't get it, that they dismiss her feelings and concerns, and she feels worse. When it's your life that's falling apart, remember that you're not the only person who is new to this. As new as widowhood was to me, it was just as new to the

---

* I am joking! This is a terrible idea, and if you are a tech genius, please do not pursue this.

people around me. As much as I hate to bear any responsibility in life, the fault was equal among myself and the people whose absences I was tallying like a deranged high school principal. It was their job to try to show up. It was my job to give them some context for what I was going through, to open the door just enough for them to get their toes in.

Not everyone is going to show up, whether on their own, or by request. That hurts, and it also helps. When someone does this—when they show us what they're capable and incapable of—then we can adjust our expectations. When someone confirms that they are doing their best, and their best is not even close to good enough, we can find people who are better suited for us. Even when the people who are disappointing us are our parents. The fact is, the people who get you through this time may not be the same people who wiped your butt when you were a baby and paid for your braces when you were a teenager. They may not be the people who signed *Love you like a sister!* in your middle school yearbook. Those people—the people who have formed the foundation of your life so far— may still be in your life, they will just take on another role. But having them step down as the pillars for your grief support leaves space for someone else—someone better suited to the role—to step in. They may not be who you thought would show up, but they'll be there. And that's what will make them the right people.

•   •   •

Easy Ways to Be Decent to a Grieving Person

If you're grieving, I recommend just taking a photo of this page and putting it passive-aggressively on your Instagram page with no added commentary.

Remember

Put their person's deathaversary, birthday, anniversary, and other milestones in your calendars. They will know when their son should have turned sixteen, or when their husband would have retired. Reaching out to them around big milestones lets people know that they aren't as alone as they may feel, but remembering that these may be tender times for them and that they may require extra patience or love or space around these dates is just as valuable.

Say Their Name

Dead people have names, too. And the sound of it on someone else's lips is like a healing, audible balm to a grieving person. Your fear says that saying their loved one's name will remind them of what they lost. They haven't forgotten their person is dead, but their greatest fear is that everyone else will forget their dead person. Saying the dead person's name reminds the griever that their person was real, and that their life mattered. Say it. Say it. Say it.

It's Not About You

Countless widows have reported good friends who are irritated that the widow hasn't responded to a brunch invite or didn't show up for the barbecue. They want to know why their friend can't get it together and just show up for a simple meal with friends, or at least remember to RSVP with their regrets. Is grief an excuse for being rude? Well, it kind of is, and confronting a grieving person over a brunch is not exactly polite conversation, either. Grief is unpredictable. The closer the loss, the harder it is to forecast how you'll feel on any given day. Remind yourself that the grieving person is going through something *really hard* that has nothing to do with you, even if it makes your brunch count uneven. Remind yourself that even though it often seems like the world revolves around you, in this case, it certainly does not.

Think Small

On my first Mother's Day without Aaron, my expectations were very low. If Aaron were alive, he and Ralph would have made me breakfast and given me a gift that Ralph had definitely not purchased. I took Facebook off my phone so I wouldn't have to see all the sweet things that my friends' partners were doing for the mothers of their children, and counted on Ralph and me just spending a quiet day together. Instead, I received a beautiful bouquet of flowers. They were from "Ralph," my then two-year-old, who did not have a credit card and did not know how to operate the internet yet. Really, they were from an anonymous person who knew that Aaron would have gotten me flowers on Mother's Day and stepped in to make sure that I got some. If you're thinking of doing something nice . . . do it. It doesn't have to be on a milestone, and it doesn't have to be flashy. You don't even have to sign your name. Drop some grocery store gift cards in their mailbox. Shovel their snow before they wake up. Donate to a relevant charity in their person's name, even (especially!) if their person died long ago. It's never too late to be thoughtful.

Antisocial Media

Not everyone wants to share their tragedy on social media. Not everyone wants to have to perform their grief for an online audience or open up their newsfeed to see their own personal heartache as filtered through the lens of friends, family, and acquaintances. A general rule: if you don't see the person *closest to* the tragedy posting about it, there is probably a reason why. Let them take the lead on how information is disseminated. You can always write your feelings in your journal instead of on Facebook. It totally counts.

About Weddings

I know weddings are emotionally loaded. I know you're thinking, *Should I even invite them? Won't being a wedding guest be* too much *for them?* Maybe! Extend the invite with a gentle caveat: we'd love to have you, and completely understand if it's too much for you. And extend the invite with a plus one. I know that weddings are expensive and we're all trying to be economical. I get that weddings are intimate, and nobody wants a stranger in their wedding photos. But if you are going to invite a widow to your wedding, at least give them the grace of a social buffer for what could be emotionally cathartic or mildly awkward. If you're really stressed out over the cost of one additional dinner setting, send the itemized invoice to TED for reimbursement.* Otherwise, give the widow a damn plus one. No exceptions. No excuses.

---

* Editor's note: Do not do this. TED will not reimburse any wedding expenses of any kind.

6 Shhh

I have a job that requires a lot of empathy: I produce a podcast that tells our subjects' most difficult stories. Many of these stories are traumatic and devastating and there is no happy ending to them. The baby dies. The wife never stops drinking. The dad never returns. What all of these stories have in common is that the person they belong to hardly ever thinks that their story is the *most* tragic, the *most* difficult. If anything, they're baffled as to what makes their story of any interest to me, or to our listeners. Why would anyone *want* to hear about the most terrible thing another person has experienced? There are many reasons; some we wouldn't even be able to identify within ourselves. We listen as a form of emotional insurance, a way to prepare for when a Very Bad Thing happens to us or to someone we love. We listen for catharsis, for relief of whatever we've been bottling up inside. We listen for voyeurism or out of curiosity, or to build and flex our empathy muscles. We listen to learn what to do when we go through something like this. Or when we know someone else is having a similar experience. Listening to a podcast about a difficult situation is easier than listening to someone's experience in real life, where there are things like eye contact and people sitting at the next table in the restaurant, casually eavesdropping. It's *much* easier when there is a pause button and a fast-forward and a gentle narrator and some well-timed music cues to let you know when to wince, when to weep.

Some of my earliest childhood memories are of sitting in the front seat of my mom's Volvo station wagon during rush hour, the setting sun beating down directly into my eyes, my mom insisting that we listen to the "jazz and traffic" station. I was aware that my mother had just spent nine hours toiling in a cubicle in order to put me and my siblings through private school, but I didn't care. I wanted her to use her commute time to entertain me. To talk to me, ask me questions about my very intriguing middle-school life. "Mom," I said one evening, "I *hate* silence. Don't you hate silence?"

My mother looked at me with a peace I hope to someday have in my heart and said, "No."

Silence, to me, was a void to be filled. I did not yet know the glory of a silent moment. The wonder of blank space. Silence is scary for many of us. We are used to keeping our bodies and minds and mouths busy at all times. Our calendars resemble multicolor checkerboards telling us where we're rushing off to next. Our relationships with our friends and family are a form of multitasking—I'll call you from the car! I'll email you while I'm walking on the treadmill! There are moments in life where all this business grinds to a sudden halt. Think of the moment when you slam on your brakes and stop just short of the bumper in front of you. The phone call you take where the bad news you never expected is delivered in a conversation that lasts just a few seconds. The birth of a child—everyone in the room waiting for that very first cry, the sound of life. The death of a loved one—the holy silence that follows that very last breath. These are moments that we do not rush to fill. Moments that seem to quickly sort the chaos out into manageable columns, that sort the real from the bullshit. These are moments where everything seems to hang in suspended animation, a blessed now where only the present is present. They are only moments—quick visions of clarity before we're snapped back into the chaos.

It's the memory of those moments that I am pursuing in the chaos of every day. A moment of clarity that I'd rather get without watching another loved one die.

I no longer hate silence. It is no longer a void waiting for my sparkling insights to fill it. It's a space where something bigger than me can happen.

When you're around a grieving person, silence feels like the enemy. It's awkward, right? Only if you believe that it's your job to fill it.

It isn't.

Remember when I said that empathy isn't about where *you* are? It's not. If the silence is awkward for you, let it be awkward.

Much of my work, even as the host and writer of the program, is just to listen. To go against all my instincts as a Midwesterner— the girl who wants to relate to you by matching you anecdote for anecdote—and let my subjects own their story.

Everyone has a certain way they tell their story. Let's say I called you on the phone today. First off, you better answer. I know when people send me to voice mail. When you answered, and I asked you to relate to me your most formative life story, you'd start where you always start. You'd tell me the same thing you always tell people, with the same story arc you've relayed to countless other people. It's the elevator pitch for your life, for your trauma, for your "getting to know you" kinda talks.

I'd let you tell me that version, and I'd ask you some questions, but I wouldn't rush to fill the silence between us. Instead, I'd let it sit there and see what develops. I'd see what *you* fill it with, how you use it to reflect on what you've said, and where you put your new reflections. You may cry, and that's okay. But I won't rush to tell you that it's going to be okay, and that you're doing great. I will not shower you with platitudes.

I will let the silence sit there.

I do not always know what to say, but I do know how to listen.

All of us can start there—with a listen. Specifically, listening just to listen, not to speak. A podcast is a good place to start if you need extra practice building that listening muscle. Even if you *wanted* to interrupt the storyteller with your own advice, your own anecdote, you cannot. Pretend, the next time you are faced with a difficult conversation you'd rather run away from, that you're listening to a podcast. That you are there for the suffering person as a pair of ears, wide open. You may utter an "mmmm" or nod enthusiastically to signal you're listening, but you do not need to jump in with your own story about your aunt's friend who died the same way, isn't that crazy? It is not crazy. It is an annoying distraction from the story at hand.

Hardly anybody intends to be rude or dismissive, but just because my dog doesn't think it's rude to sneeze directly into my mouth doesn't make it okay that she does it. I have had many conversations about grief where I felt like I'd been force-fed a spoonful of sugar when all I needed was the medicine of actually being seen and heard through my dark time. All I needed was for someone to say, "That's really hard," and then shut their own mouth while I unleashed the torrent of thoughts that had been pent up in my mind since my last adult interaction.

"Nora," you may be thinking, *"isn't that what therapy is for?"* Yes! And it is also for interpersonal relationships that do not rely on an insurance co-pay. If you've ever had your friends sit through a diatribe about your quest for the perfect bridesmaid dress, or talked their ear off about your homebrewing kit, or unpacked the minutiae of your terrible boss's worst behaviors, you can sit through a one-sided conversation about their divorce, their disease, or the death of their loved one.

There is no hot dish that can cure a broken heart or a dead person. We cannot cure one another or keep each other from suffering. But we can listen, and that's a start.

•   •   •

Grievers, while I would highly recommend these pages be illegally photocopied and sprinkled outside of every funeral home in your area, the best way to teach people what to say or not to say is the best way to teach anything: positive reinforcement. When someone says something wonderfully comforting to you (or even just not *discomfiting*), tell them! Tell them: "That was really nice to hear. Thank you."

A Form Letter for When You Don't Know What to Say

When you don't know what to write, choose from these options!

GREETING

Dear (Name of Griever),

Hello (Name of Griever),

CONDOLENCE

I'm so sorry to hear about (Name of Dead Person).

I was so sad to hear about (Name of Dead Person).

KIND GESTURE

One of my favorite memories of (Name of Dead Person) is: (a memory that doesn't involve sex, drugs, or illegal activities, unless that is just a part of the dead person's legacy, in which case, stay true to their memory!).

I've enclosed a check for your family to use for whatever you like. Please don't send a thank-you note, you have enough to do.

CLOSING

Sincerely, (Your Name Here—remember to write your own name)

With love, (Me—again, write your actual name, not just me)

Things You Should Not Say to a Person Who Is Grieving

If you're thinking any of these things, remember that talking is always completely optional.

"Could be worse."

Could be better, too! But the current status of a person's feelings is not up for debate.

"To put this in perspective . . ."

Everyone has a perspective. This may not be a very wide one, but it's still valid. Being close to something—having your grief so close it makes your eyes cross—is still a perspective. Unless someone on the ground specifically *asks* about your view from thirty thousand feet, let them talk from where they are right now. They need to.

"Here's what you need to do."

Unless you've been exactly where I am, I don't want to hear where you think I should go. Unless I specifically asked you for your advice, I do not want to hear it.

"For what it's worth ..."

I just said I didn't want to hear your advice! Stop trying to sneak it in!

"You're so strong."

I know this sounds like a compliment, and I know you mean it as one, but you don't know how strong someone is, you only know how strong they look. And hearing this as a compliment makes them feel like strength is their only option. Like exposing their weakness would not be as admirable.

"Everything happens for a reason."

False.

7 To Do

Grief is so much work. Not just the emotional work, but the *paperwork*. Death comes with a long to-do list, and even years later you can find yourself thinking, *Are you* kidding *me? I thought I took care of this!* There's no universal checklist for what needs to get done, but there are some general tips that will make the drudgery of death slightly less *terrible*.

• • •

1. Order as many death certificates as you can afford. You have no idea how hard it is to prove someone is dead until your person dies. Where I live, the first death certificate was free (score!) and the rest were available for a fee. It wasn't cheap, but I ordered fifty just to be considerate of Future Nora, who I knew would not want to go down to the government center in five or ten or twenty-five years to dig up a death certificate on a busy Wednesday. I flew through these, and now Future Nora will likely have to go and get some more death certificates at some point. I had to provide them to Aaron's cell phone carrier, his student loan company, our bank, his bank, the sperm bank that was holding his frozen sperm, and to countless other entities, most of whom didn't bother returning them. Rude.

2. Pretend death paperwork is a (nonpaying, part-time, no-benefits) job. Devote a part of your day to chipping away a little at a time. Apologies to your actual employer, but this will need to be done during business hours because you're going to have to spend a lot of time on the phone, talking to various customer service representatives and their direct supervisors, all of whom will tell you something different. Keep a pillow in your cubicle to scream into between calls.

3. A lot of this paperwork is honest-to-goodness paper of the wood-pulp variety. You know what feels good about paper? Putting it in a nicely organized, brand-new binder from your favorite office supply store. Death and grief are chaos. A three-ring binder is order and beauty. You deserve order and beauty.

4. At least one hundred times during this process you'll think to yourself, *When I die, I won't . . .* You can fill in that blank however you like, but make sure you fill that blank in *legally*. If your dead person left their estate a mess, meet with an estate lawyer *now*. If your dead person left their house like an episode of *Hoarders*, Marie Kondo˙ your life immediately. If their death triggered any ideas about how you don't want to die, take care of that notion before you're dead. You don't want to make the same messes and

---

* Marie Kondo wrote *The Life-Changing Magic of Tidying Up* and she is why your friends are posting so many photos of their sparsely decorated homes and drawers of perfectly folded T-shirts.

mistakes your loved one made. You want to make new, exciting messes and mistakes for your loved ones to sift through!

5. Death is expensive. Unless your loved one left specific directions to bury them in a gold-plated casket, none of the stuff that they try to sell you at a funeral home is actually necessary. We buried my dad in a pine box (per his request) and dumped Aaron's ashes in his favorite river (unless you are from the Minnesota government, in which case, no we didn't). Here is something I didn't know about death bills: not all the bills you get need to be paid right away! Truly, even the most coldhearted corporate health system will let you do a payment plan. Does that feel weird, putting someone's death on layaway? Well, it shouldn't, because the people who run hospitals and health insurance companies swim in pools of money, à la Scrooge McDuck. They'll get their money eventually, but you don't need to go broke or crazy getting it to them.

6. Let someone help you. I hated this part, because accepting help felt like putting a stick in my eye, but oh my gosh! Letting someone help you is a gift to *them*. If someone really feels like coming over and sorting through piles of bills and labeling them, or calling the hospital and impersonating you while they negotiate a payment plan? LET THEM DO IT! If the bill-paying is a soothing part of your life, but you need someone to help you coordinate all the things you need help

with? Pick one person you trust, one person who is actually going to be there for you, and tell them they're in charge of wrangling all the potential do-gooders in your life. You might run out of stuff you need done. This person can make up new stuff! Or think of stuff you'd never think of! You can even make up a fancy title for them. Your Grief Captain? Your Grief Manager? The name is your call.

7. Talk to someone. For many people, the idea of going to a therapist is laughable. Paying someone to talk about my feelings? Ha! For many people, the idea of going to a therapist is also economically impossible. Paying someone *how much* to talk about my feelings? I wish! The Hot Young Widows Club was established because I wasn't willing to see a therapist and I wasn't excited about the idea of sitting in a circle and talking about my grief. I've since changed my position on both of those notions, but the point is, you have *options*. Sometimes it seems like shoving your feelings deep down inside and smothering them with a bottle of wine and a box of cookies is the best option. But like anyone who avoids taking out the kitchen garbage by just shoving the contents a little farther down can tell you . . . that only works for so long. To this day, my mother has not seen a grief counselor or a therapist after losing my dad and Aaron, and I fully expect her to emotionally implode any day now. I don't care if it's a Facebook group, a faith leader, or a professional therapist, I promise you that you need to talk to someone about what you've been through. Not just your friends and your family,

but a neutral third party who can help you sort through the tangle of feelings lodged in your chest.

8. Take. It. Slow. This is a not a race, and there is no award for being the Fastest Griever. You can't rush your way through this, and you can't be rushed through it. If your body is tired, take a nap. If you don't want to go out to dinner with your friends, cancel. If ever there were a time for you to slow down and expect less from yourself: this is it. Your new goal is to become an underachiever. To do only the bare minimum.

9. A person is not the things they owned. My father said this to me constantly when I was younger because, like all children, I was a borderline hoarder. Aaron left behind several giant plastic bins filled with action figures, five guitars (!!!!), and over three hundred novelty T-shirts from bands I have never heard of. I kept some of it. I donated some of it. I threw some of it in the trash. I gave some to our friends and family. You can let go of the thing without letting go of the person. My dad told me that way before Marie Kondo ever wrote that book, by the way. They were both right.

10. Get a journal. I don't care if you only write two words a day. This part of your life is going to be a blur, and you'll look back at your grief-thoughts someday and think, *Who wrote this?* Nothing can show you how far you've come better than a physical documentation of the lowest parts of your life.

8 To Not Do

Like everything I judge other people for saying, I have said it myself countless times to people in grief:

"Take care of yourself!"

As if, when your world is crashing down around you, you'll find the time to put on a face mask and curl up with a good book and a cup of tea. As if, when your heart aches so much you think it might actually be breaking, you'll think, *I should go get a massage*.

Self-care is a hot buzzword right now. Depending on who you ask, it means anything from being halfway decent to yourself, to outright spoiling yourself. Or, to use the worst word that has ever been invented, "pampering" yourself with treats like manicures, pedicures, and Netflix marathons.

Everyone urged me to take care of myself after Aaron died. I nodded and smiled at their recommendations and promised to do that, but I had no idea what they meant. Looking back, I can confidently say that they did not mean, "You should drink a bottle of Skinnygirl Margarita tonight and fall asleep at two in the morning!" Or, "Eat a bag of peanut butter M&M's for lunch!"

I'd love to make this chapter a simple list of the ways you could be nice to yourself, but I don't think that matters. In the words o my friend Sarah Super, a rape survivor and activist, "Sometimes there aren't enough kale salads in the world to heal us."

Not to knock a nice kale salad, but the most important way I found to take care of myself was to stop taking care of other people and their grief. Because that's a hard truth that follows death: the closer you are to a loss, the more likely you are to become a depository for the grief of other people.

When my friend's child died, her aunt told her, "I just don't know how I'll survive this."

When another friend's husband died, her friend told her, "You know, you're not helping me with my grief."

A few months after Aaron died, I got an email whose subject line read, *Pay attention to me!!!*, the contents of which admonished me for not replying to a previous email.

We should know better than to do or say these things to each other, but we apparently don't, because every grieving person I've ever met has a similar story: the woman whose estranged sister shows up to her husband's funeral demanding forgiveness for a decades-old fight, the nephew who resurfaces to ask for money he was promised from Grandma before she died.

The closer you are to a loss, the more likely you are to be totally, emotionally shipwrecked, and the more likely you are to be pulled under by people whose boats were barely even rocked.

In the months after Aaron died, I ran myself into the ground trying to make everyone else feel okay. I had lunch with people I didn't even like, and I gave Aaron's things to people *he* didn't even like. I tried my best to smooth any rough edges, to make Aaron's death as frictionless as possible for people who, by and

laugh, had not been there for Aaron's long good bye. I watched
Moe do the same thing: I watched her comfort others when she
herself needed comfort, and watched her smile through things
that she later screamed and cried about.

Being forced to guide other people through their grief
happens in subtle ways—coffees you don't want to meet for,
texts you don't want to read from someone you don't want to
deal with. These things eat away at your limited time and energy
until you don't have enough left over to take care of yourself.
It's hard to say no to people when you are suffering. You're
defenseless, skinless. You don't want people to think that death
has hardened you. But it has, at least a little bit, for at least a
little while. There is nothing unkind about prioritizing yourself.
I don't care if you never take a bubble bath, or if you never do a
single yoga pose. The most important way you can take care of
yourself right now is to stop saying yes to the shit you don't want
to do.

How to Set a Boundary When You're Grieving

A list of things that would not be recommended by any licensed therapist, but are endorsed by me through my own anecdotal research.

Ghost

Look, I will frown upon this in nearly any other social situation. I'll tell you that you need to just admit to your date you're not interested in seeing them again, or have that hard conversation with your former best friend. But you are a grieving person, and you've got a lot going on, and you are not obligated to reply to every single text message and email you get. The wonderful thing about technology is that it keeps us in touch with people. The horrible thing about technology is that it gives people constant access to us, when we just want to curl up alone. I hereby grant you permission to simply not reply to every piece of correspondence you receive. To just . . . not.

Ghost more elegantly

Okay, there is one more redeeming part of technology: it allows us to communicate hard things to a lot of people, all at once. Whatever your preferred mode of contact (email, Facebook, or something that hasn't been invented at the time of this writing), use it to tell people when you need some space. It doesn't have to be long, it just has to remind people that they have no idea what you're going through, and not to take it personally.

Here, I wrote one for you:

> Hi, friends. I'm overwhelmed with, and grateful for, all your love and support. If I haven't responded to your messages lately, please be patient with me. I haven't done this before, and I need time and space to process everything on my own. xoxo

Now even your most exhausting family member won't take it personally when you're not at their beck and call, even though it's totally personal.

Be up front

The emotionally mature thing to do is of course the hardest one, and the one furthest on my list. If the person is close enough to you to be worth this effort, if they're someone you truly want in your life when this tempest has calmed down a little, you have to tell them the truth. If they're decent, they'll understand. If they're like most people, good luck with that conversation.

9 At Least

A partial list of word pairings that don't belong together:

- fat free
- just relax
- half sibling
- at least

Those are in no particular order, but that last one is a really annoying combination for anyone who has been through anything. Whatever follows those two words is never going to offer comfort to another person. It's a subtle way of saying, "I'm about to say something sanctimonious to you, so get ready to tune me out."

I hadn't noticed it before, how those two syllables can be weaponized so stealthily that the speaker doesn't know the damage they've done.

And then Aaron died.

I knew from watching other people go through hard things that the suffering of others is often insufferable for everyone else. It's very hard to watch someone struggle, and it's not unusual for us to want other people to just get over it already. Saying "get over it" is unequivocally rude; we could *never* say that! So we'll say whatever words are adjacent to that same phrase, but seem a lot less harsh.

"At least his suffering is over."

"At least you have Ralph."

"At least you got to fall in love once."

The hidden message in all of these "at least" sentences is this:

"Whatever you're sad about makes me deeply uncomfortable, so I'd like to point out all the things you aren't being grateful for right now." As a former Catholic, this is a very real fear in my life. I avoided having birthday parties my entire life because a gathering of friends and family could not outweigh the anxiety provoked by the idea of opening gifts in front of an audience who may not find me sufficiently grateful for what I received.

If ever you could earn a pass for just Being Bummed Out, it would be the year after your husband dies of cancer at age thirty-five, right? Wrong. People didn't want me to be sad, they wanted me to triumph over my sadness. They wanted me to inspire them, dammit! I found myself self-editing my feelings for the sake of strangers on the internet, posting things that would acknowledge that I was lucky to find Aaron, and sad to lose him. On one such photo, where I'd read and reread the caption to make sure I struck the right balance between grief and gratitude, I got this comment:

> At least you got to fall in love. Some people never get that. Be grateful for the love you had.
> —an actual Instagram comment from a stranger

Those two words confirmed my biggest fear: that I was not grateful enough, that I had to do better. It was my job to get through this misery as quickly as possible for the sake of everyone who crossed my path on- or offline.

I am a person who enjoys finding the silver lining on my storm clouds, but I'm also aware that sometimes, they're harder to spot. Sometimes, they don't appear at all. And sometimes, there is no sunny side of the street. Sometimes, it's just a monsoon of Terrible, and all we can do is hold on and wait for the storm to pass.

When you're in the midst of a crisis, pawing your way through the dark, the last thing you need is for someone to tell you to look on the bright side. It is okay for some things to just be bad. It is okay for some things to just be hard. It is not our job to wrestle a big life lesson out of every hurt we are dealt, or to find that lesson in a hurry.

If there's anything people love more than a happy story, it's a sad story with a happy ending. We love to see someone destroy their demons, overcome oppression, pull themselves up by their bootstraps. We love to see the hero get knocked down twice and get up three times. The math doesn't even need to make sense. We just want to see that even the insurmountable is . . . surmountable. We are thirsty, all of us, for an ice-cold glass of lemonade made from the lemons life hurls at each of us.

As a person who is still holding her breath for a Lindsay Lohan comeback, I deeply understand this compulsion. I spent the year after my husband's and father's deaths pretending to be okay for anyone and everyone. I was inspiration porn for anyone going through adversity. My husband may be dead, but my lipstick was on, my outfits were perfect, and my selfies were hot fire.

Whatever my Instagram feed told the world, the truth was that I was far from okay. I hardly slept. I drank too much. I forgot to eat. I wasn't taking care of myself, but I sure looked like I was. I looked great. I made it look easy. I was a comeback story, and I hadn't even taken any time off.

I wasn't doing that because anybody *told* me to snap back and get my act together quickly. I was doing it because I myself had turned away from enough sad stories to know that culturally, Americans have a hard time giving people time to suffer, time to grieve. We are okay with the suffering of others if and only if there is a clean resolution at the end, preferably with a lesson learned.

How boring to expect a clean, concise, and swift resolution to something like *life*. In Tana Toraja, an island in eastern Indonesia, the dead person is embalmed and kept in the family's home. The dead body is dressed, offered food, and treated as if they are ill, until the funeral. The funeral is a huge feast that lasts for six days. The family has spent years saving up for this event.* In Madagascar, millions of people practice *Famadihana*, a ritual where the dead are periodically exhumed for a celebration that includes dancing, telling the story of the dead, and maintaining a connection between who is here, and who came before.**

* https://ideas.ted.com/11-fascinating-funeral-traditions-from-around-the-globe

** https://archive.nytimes.com/www.nytimes.com/2010/09/06/world/africa/06madagascar.html

And then there's America. The average American gets three days of bereavement leave when they lose a spouse. They get three for a parent, or a sibling. They get three for a child.* If you lose your best friend? Your boyfriend? If you lose your favorite uncle? If you lose a spouse to divorce, or if the fertilized egg never implants? I suppose you could take PTO.

Of course, this is assuming you work a full-time job with benefits. If you're hourly, or contract, or work in the service industry . . . you're on your own. We do not have a policy for you, or for your bereavement.

The point here is not just that our Western culture has somehow calculated an official amount of days for you to quickly work through your grief before returning to your desk, it's that we have very little guidance in general when it comes to grief. If you're lucky enough to be from a culture that holds space for grief—if you sit shiva, or wear white for a year after your husband dies—you still have to contend with an entire country that believes the words *bereavement* and *policy* do not belong anywhere near each other.

In other words, it is okay to suffer and be sad if you come out the other end as a new and improved version of yourself. Maybe that's where you are right now, wondering what Best Self will emerge from this hell. Surely that Best Self must be around here somewhere? Maybe underneath the raw, angry person you are right now? Maybe. And maybe not.

Maybe, sometimes, hard things are just hard. Maybe the standard for suffering shouldn't be Enlightenment and Improvement, but simply surviving. Because even surviving is not

---

* https://www.shrm.org/ResourcesAndTools/business-solutions/Documents/
   Paid-Leave-Report-All-Industries-All-FTEs.pdf

a given. If you've been on social media at all in the past few years, you may have noticed that crowdfunding has moved beyond financially supporting our friend's kooky inventions and ill-conceived film ideas and into the equally devastating terrain of funding everything from IVF to cancer treatment to funeral expenses.

Most Americans do not have five hundred dollars to cover an emergency.* Medical emergencies are *always* going to cost more than five hundred dollars, that's what makes them emergencies! If you don't have five hundred dollars for a medical emergency, you've now added a financial emergency to your list of problems.

Why are widows more likely than married people to experience heart failure?

Because sometimes, the things that don't kill us *don't* make us stronger. Sometimes they ruin us spiritually, emotionally, financially, and physically.

But that's not a very palatable story, is it?

We need the unpalatable story. We need to know that sometimes, the worst thing that happens to us is *not* a catalyst for creating something bigger. Sometimes, when God closes a door, she also nails shut all the windows, too.

The pressure to be good at grief is too much to add to your full plate. Maybe right now, it just hurts. It's just *hard*. If your life has fallen apart, I am here to give you the opposite advice of every sympathy card or empty platitude that will be handed to you over the coming days:

No matter how many lemons life gives you, you don't owe anyone a glass of lemonade.

* http://money.cnn.com/2017/01/12/pf/americans-lack-of-savings/index.html

How to Tell the People You Love That You're Not Okay

Stop Lying

That sounds harsh, but you are a liar. We all are. I know that we all say, "How are you?" as a reflexive greeting to one another, but if you give the same answer to your siblings as you do to the cashier at Walgreens you're going to get the same response, which is small talk. You cannot keep everyone in your life at a surface level and survive this. In order to be there for you, the people who love you need to know the whole truth. They need you to say, "I am doing very poorly, and I can't quite tell you what I need from you, I just need you to know that."

Before you can stop lying to other people, you need to ask if you're being totally honest with yourself. Are you taking care of yourself? Are you giving yourself time to just exist? Or are you jam-packing your days with activities in order to avoid your feelings? How are you, really? Write it down if you need to see it to believe it. And the next time someone you love asks you, give them the real answer.

Pick a Messenger

So you're not okay. You don't have to put all your business out there for everyone in the world. Pick a person in your life you trust, and have them be your point person, the messenger who tells people how you're doing and what you need. Maybe this is your Grief Captain (are we liking that name, or no?), but maybe it's just someone who is really good at communicating things.

Pick a Preferred Communication Mode

Not all of us are built for blogs and Facebook updates. I used email to send as much information as I could, to as many people as I could, without having to interact with all of them. An email could let people know what I was going through and what I needed. Did I forget to put some people on it? Yes. Was that okay? Also yes. You don't need to be perfect at this.

10 Why Do You Ask?

People always talk about how curious cats are, but cats seem pretty good at minding their own business. I've never had a cat ask me what size my jeans are, or how tall I am. A cat has never asked me how my husband got brain cancer or if I'm afraid Ralph will have it one day. A cat has never asked if I worry what people think about me "moving on." *People* ask these questions. They ask tons of questions about widowhood, and death, and motherhood. Because *people* are the curious ones.

People want to know all kinds of things. People asked Moe if her husband showed any signs of being suicidal. They asked me if Aaron gave me "permission" to remarry after his death. They asked my friend why she gave birth to a baby who would only live a few months anyway, and another friend if her marriage ended because of infidelity. All of these questions seem, to me at least, like questions that would be better off not being asked. But each of the people who asked these questions believed that this was information they needed, and information they should gather.

People *are* curious.

The unkind part of me hears questions like these and thinks, *What is wrong with you?!*

The kinder part of me hears questions like these and thinks, *I know what you really want to know.*

What you—what they, these askers of probing, personal questions—want to know is that what happened was not an anomaly. It was not senseless. It happened for an identifiable reason, one that they can protect themselves from. These questions are designed to put a little distance between the asker and what happened. People are asking these questions not just for their own curiosity, but for their own safety. They want to know if my friend's son was drinking before he drowned because they want to believe that there has to be a solid reason for a tragedy to strike. A reason helps them cross off this specific tragedy from the list of possible life tragedies that may befall their family. Their son would *never* swim drunk, which makes them safe. Right? They want to know if Moe's husband showed signs of suicide, so they can look at their own partner and say, "This could never happen to us." They want to believe that Aaron's brain cancer was hereditary (it wasn't), so they know it could never happen to their son, or their spouse (it can). As much as we know that tragedy comes for us all, we're desperate to believe that it will maybe skip us over. That we can will tragedy to forget about us and move on to someone else. Someone who smokes or drinks or texts while they drive. Which we, of course, would *never* do.

It's such a nice and comforting thought that if we ask the right questions, we can save ourselves from a lifetime of suffering. I get it. I have asked plenty of questions I wish I could take back. Questions that, on reflection, were just trying to bubble wrap me from the possibility that I may also experience suffering someday. When I heard about an acquaintance's baby being born with a genetic disorder, I looked at my then-boyfriend skeptically, trying to imagine what was lurking in his genetic code. "Do you or anyone in your family have any history I should know about?" I casually asked one night. "You know, anything you want to tell me before we get married and have babies?" We never got married or had babies. I broke up with him, in part because he lived very unhealthily. He drank, he smoked, he never worked out, he ate like a garbage can. I married Aaron—a man who had never done one single illegal drug, had never smoked a single cigarette. A man who ran a marathon and played adult recreational sports several times a week. That unhealthy ex-boyfriend of mine is still very much alive. Aaron died of brain cancer three years after we said "I do."

●   ●   ●

"Why do you ask?"

This is a response for a question you don't want to answer, a way of giving yourself a little bit of space, and forcing a little bit of reflection on your inquisitor. It's also a question to consider before you ask.

Why *do* you ask?

Are you asking a question for you own knowledge? To satisfy your own curiosity? If so, could your curiosity be sated with a Google search later on?

If you're asking because you're trying to make conversation, and you remember from your high school etiquette class that a question is a surefire way to keep a conversation going, what else could you ask about? What will asking this particular question actually add to the conversation?

If I were you and read the previous few pages, I'd probably be picking up my phone and blocking myself from contacting anyone but my immediate family, just in case I ever put my foot in my mouth. The fear of saying the wrong thing can be so crippling that it can become easier to just say nothing at all. To simply disappear from the conversation, or from the relationship, in an effort to save everyone the embarrassment of a mishap.

You do not need to be the perfect Grief Conversationalist. You do not need to approach every single suffering person with the correct healing words. I firmly believe that saying the wrong thing is better than saying nothing at all. Saying the wrong thing is, at least, a sign that you tried. There is no algorithm for empathy and understanding. There is no formula or conversation script that will fit every situation. There is no substitute for human effort and error, for learning with one another.

I learned from every dumb thing that was said to me after Aaron died. I learned that when the topic of my dead husband comes up, which it often does, because I love Aaron and talk about him all the time, people freeze for at least a moment while their brains struggle to come up with a response. They've just heard me say that my husband died at age thirty-five. Their brain has highlighted a few words. *Died. Thirty-five.* Their brain makes some computer noises and comes up with some natural next questions.

"How did he die?"

"Were there any signs?"

What is easy to miss out on is this word: *husband*. A partner. A deep love. In any other context, what would we want to know about the person someone has chosen to spend their life with?

"How did you meet your husband?"

"What was your husband like?"

"What did your husband do?"

We are used to following the shocking line of the story. It's a disturbance in the force when a person dies young, but even a dead young person is not just their death. We can train ourselves to be curious not just about the sad part of the story, but about the hero of the story.

The profile for a recent conference I attended included a prompt to fill in.

Ask me about:

I wrote, *my dead husband*.

Not to shock, but because I love to talk about Aaron. I love to talk about his *life*. Not because questions about his death will bring up unpleasant memories, but because I want the chance to pull up my best memories of him, a chance to set aside the list of medications he took, his schedule of brain surgeries and radiation appointments, and talk about his love, his partnership, and the way I carry him with me still.

When we meet, I don't want Aaron to be a sad story for you. I want him to be a love story and a life story with a little side dish of sadness. I want to talk about Aaron the way you talk about your partner—living or dead. I want to connect over the magic of love, not just the trauma of death.

Think of the worst thing that happened to you so far. Maybe it's death. Maybe it's a lost job. A divorce. Did it help define you? Of course. Is it your defining feature? I hope not. Because we are the sum of our experiences and our interactions.

I want to know about the big thing in your life, but only as much as it tells me about *you*. The what and the how aren't nearly as interesting to me as what comes next: the why. *Why* does this event matter to you, and where has it brought you? How has it bolstered you, undone you? When you push the bruise of that time in your life, do you still feel the sting, and do you kind of like it?

I'll tell you anything you want to know about my life, and my loss, but you could google all the details and get just as clear a picture of what happened factually. Two people fell in love. One got sick and died. But a list of facts doesn't tell you who those facts made me into, or where I'm going.

You can ask me anything—just make sure you know why you're asking.

A List of Topics If You're About to See a Grieving Person:

The weather

Just kidding! You can do better than that. But man, can you believe this snow?

A favorite memory you have of the dead person

Remember that time you all went tubing down the river? Or the time they camped out to get concert tickets for you? Sometimes, the awfulness of death can cloud the best memories of who a person was. Having some of those memories returned to you can be a gift. Having the opportunity to share *your* favorite parts of a dead person you love is even better.

A trait you admired in the dead person

Think of all the nice things you say about someone behind their back. Now say it to the face of someone who loves them. We all see different things in different people. Seeing our loved ones through someone else's eyes is like seeing a whole new version of them.

A confession

I have no idea what to say. But I wanted you to know that I'm thinking of you.

11 Who Gets to Grieve?

It was raining when Prince died. I remember this not because I'm a die-hard Prince fan, but because "Purple Rain" was playing when I started my car. The song is nearly ten minutes long, and I love every minute of it. When it ended, I switched stations, and it was playing there, too. I flipped through all of my presets, and all of them were playing "Purple Rain." *Wow*, I thought, *this is a story that will only be interesting to me when I try to repeat it in the future.*

Eventually, a DJ came on to announce Prince's death. That night, Minneapolis's First Avenue held an all-night dance party for Prince. The streets of downtown were filled with his fans, many of them weeping.

Somewhere, Prince's inner circle was grieving, too. Not because an icon was gone, but because their friend, their family member, was gone. What did they think of all these regular people getting Prince tattoos and crying publicly? Was it a comfort to them, or an annoyance?

No matter the level of fame a person achieves in their life, every death has a ripple effect. Every death brings grief out of unexpected places. Aaron's funeral had over a thousand attendees. I do not personally know a thousand people, and I could not tell you the names of most of the people who were there. But it was comforting to know that his life had meant enough to this many people that they would come out on a cold winter night to say good-bye to the man I loved, that they had loved him in their own way, too.

The magic of grief is that it can make our broken hearts bigger. That night, I loved everyone in that room. I loved the grade-school acquaintances of his, and the former co-workers. I loved the estranged cousins!

I will also confess that some public displays of grief pushed all the wrong buttons in me. They made me angry, which made me feel Grinchy, which made me feel awful about myself.

That is the black magic of grief: it can make our broken hearts smaller and meaner.

People are a nonrenewable resource (as of this writing, I'm sure someone is working on reanimating corpses to make sure we live forever). Sometimes it feels like grief is, too. Like there is only so much of it to go around.

A friend of mine was angry because when her brother died their very distant stepsister, whom they had never lived with and barely knew, got a huge memorial tattoo. "He's MY brother," she texted me, "and he didn't even like her!"

There is a highly subjective difference between people who are simply tenderhearted and easily affected by another person's death, and a Grief Vulture. But both are real, and both tend to show up in the wake of a person's death.

Tender Person characteristics:

- cries at sad commercials
- has never killed a fly
- hurts for you
- gives you a melancholy feeling
- the human version of a peeled orange

Grief Vulture characteristics:

- chronic oversharer
- ratio of relationship with dead person to social media shares is 1:10
- wants to know too much about your own grief
- gives you an ick feeling
- human version of a vulture, duh

How you see these people is a direct reflection of how you feel. And that's okay. Because grief does real things to your heart. At your best, you will see every sad person as a tender one. You will see the best in them and in their intentions. And they will usually be worth it. At your worst, you will see people circling your grief like it's emotional carrion. It will make you feel defensive and angry. You will want to comment on their posts and write, *But you weren't even a good cousin to her!*

Don't do that. Even if it's true.

I saw a lot of vultures after Aaron died. I was angry at the number of people who had disappeared during his illness and were reappearing to grieve him. How dare they elicit sympathy for a loss they didn't have a claim to. How dare they waste other people's empathy on their own, empty grief.

My in-box is filled with people who are going through the worst time in their life. They are experiencing profound losses, and these losses are compounded by the often mystifying behaviors of people they considered friends and family. The mystification is quickly and easily replaced with anger, because what the heck are they thinking?

Why did your father-in-law insist on spreading the ashes of his estranged son in a place that didn't reflect his son's clearly written wishes? Why didn't your cousin come to Grandma's funeral? Why are your parents arguing over the songs that will play at your dead sister's funeral? Why did your co-worker wear sweatpants to your husband's funeral?

Death is hard for everyone. Even your terrible uncle. Even your annoying co-worker. Death makes us all smaller and more pathetic. Yes, sometimes it makes us kinder and more patient, but it just as easily brings out the worst in terrible people, and the worst in good people, too.

So let me say to you what I would say to me if time travel were a thing:

Who cares?

Who cares if their intentions are good and tender, or desperate and slimy? What does it truly matter to you, or to your grief?

What makes you an expert on identifying crocodile tears from the real deal? If you are a crocodile expert, please think of that as a rhetorical question. If you haven't noticed this yet, people are weird. Sometimes the death of one person opens a door inside us we didn't even know existed, and a bunch of dysfunctional feelings are released. I've cried harder at the funerals of total strangers than I have at the funerals of close family members. I've been deeply, emotionally affected by the face of a person on the bus. We don't know, truly, what is happening in the hearts of others. We can only trust that it's as beautiful and complicated and confusing as what's happening in our own weird little hearts.

Someone else's grief—genuine or performative—has nothing to do with you, or with your grief. They cannot siphon off the grief from your tank of sadness. They are not drawing from a limited supply of empathy or sympathy, taking what you deserve. All these annoyances of yours are real, and they serve a real purpose: they're a nice distraction from your grief. Because it doesn't really matter what someone wears to the funeral, or who posts what on Facebook. It doesn't really matter that the co-worker you like the least showed up late to the wake he wasn't even invited to. But it feels better to be angry than it does to be bone-crushingly sad. When you're raw and vulnerable, focusing your eyes into laser beams and burning everything in your path feels way better than crying your eyes out.

Some of these things really *are* messed up. Your uncle should not have emptied your grandmother's bank account right after her death; your sister-in-law shouldn't have stolen her brother's ashes from the wake. But right now—in the thick of it?—you can't tell the difference between a misdemeanor and a felony. As a person with a deep thirst for swift justice, I understand the inclination to flip the heck out on whoever crosses you right now. As a person who talks a lot about the meditation she only does sometimes, I have a better idea for you:

List all the weird, terrible, or inappropriate things that have happened since your tragedy happened. Be detailed. Write them out in your journal (Did I tell you to get a journal yet? You need a journal). Forget about this journal entry entirely, and then find it in a few years. Read this entry with fascination. You forgot about most of these infractions! Most of these bizarre things that are grinding your gears and perhaps even your teeth will look like this: a bunch of sad, hurt people doing things they didn't realize were hurtful because they were so focused on their own pain.

The payoff for this exercise may take months, or even years, but you'll see it eventually. Millions of grievers for Prince could not take anything from the people who knew him best. A thousand people missing Aaron didn't actually take anything from me, or from him.

Anyone can be sad. Anyone can grieve. Even a vulture.

Repeat after me:

Their grief has nothing to do with my grief.

Also repeat after me:

I am now logging off social media.

12 Why Am I Still So Sad?

For the Grieving:

I quit my job just a few months after Aaron died. It made sense in the moment, but I realized that I did need money in order to keep my son and myself alive, so I went to a networking event to hopefully make some connections that would help me make money and support my child. I was introduced to a successful woman in her early seventies whom everyone referred to as a "legend." She wanted to meet me for coffee and I thought, *What could she possibly see in me?*

What she saw in me was herself. She had been sixteen when her boyfriend died. He was her first love, and they were teenagers in a different era, when it was perfectly plausible that you would be married after high school. Instead, he went to the hospital one day and never came back. She learned later that he had died of cancer, which his parents had kept secret from him and from his friends. They didn't know how to talk about it, and they didn't want him or his friends to worry.

This boy had died decades ago. She was married. She was a mother and a grandmother. And she told me about his death as if it had happened just weeks ago, as if she were still sixteen, still shocked and confused that her beloved was gone, and she'd not had a chance to say good-bye.

Her grief felt fresher than mine did, because I didn't feel anything yet.

Time is irrelevant to grief. I cannot tell you that it will feel better or worse as time goes by; I can just tell you that it feels better and worse as time goes by. The only guarantee is that however you feel right now, you will not always feel this way.

There are days when Aaron's death feels so fresh that I cannot believe it. How can he be gone? How can it be that he will forever be thirty-five years old? Likewise, there are days when his death feels like such a fact of my life I can hardly believe that he was ever *not* dead. I thought I would be able to control the faucets of my emotions. That certain days (his birthday, his deathaversary) would be drenched in meaning, and most days would not.

I wish that were the case. I wish we could relegate all our heaviest grieving to specific days of the year. It would certainly be more efficient. Instead, I know that I have some friends who will understand perfectly when I call them to say that the entire world feels heavy, that I have been crying for reasons I can't quite explain other than that I am alive and Aaron is not, and the reality of that happened to hit me in the deodorant aisle, when I spotted Aaron's favorite antiperspirant. I bought a stick for myself, so that my armpits and his armpits would be forever connected.

In 2017, Lady Gaga released her *Joanne* album, named for an aunt who died before she was even born. The titular song is 100 percent guaranteed to make you cry, and it's written about someone Lady Gaga never even met. In her Netflix documentary, *Gaga: Five Foot Two*, she plays the song for her grandmother and bawls uncontrollably. Her grandmother listens to the song, watches Gaga weep, and thanks her for the song. She does not shed a tear. Their grief—even for the same person—is different. The roots of grief are boundless. They can reach back through generations. They are undeterred by time, space, or any other law you try to apply to them.

A common adage is that "time heals all wounds." It is true physically, which I am grateful for because I am typing this while hoping the tip of my thumb fuses back together after an unfortunate kitchen accident involving me attempting to cook a potato. It is not true mentally, or emotionally. Time is cruel. Time reminds me of how long Aaron has been gone, which isn't a comfort to me.

The woman I met for coffee had lived far more of her life without that boyfriend than she had with him. Her grandchildren were now the same age she had been when she lost him. Time had not healed that wound, and it never will.

If you're still sad, that's because it's still real. They are still real. Time can change you, and it will. But it can't change them, and it won't.

●   ●   ●

For the Grief Adjacent:

For you, time marches on, steadily and reliably. A year is just a year. A day is just a day. You are not aware of the number of days it's been since they took their last breath or said their last word. You're not mentally calculating when the scales of time tip, and more of your life has been lived without them than was lived with them.

You may be tempted to tell the aggrieved to move on. After all, it's been weeks. Years. Decades. Surely this cannot still be the topic of conversation. Surely, at this point, they must have moved on?

Nope.

But, you may be thinking, this person has gotten married again, or had another baby! They have so many good things in their life, this one awful thing can't possibly *still* be relevant . . . can it?

We do not move on from the dead people we love, or the difficult situations we've lived through. We move forward, but we carry it all with us. Some of it gets easier to bear, some of it will always feel Sisyphean. We live on, but we are not the same as we once were. This is not macabre or depressing or abnormal. We are shaped by the people we love, and we are shaped by their loss.

Why are they still sad? you may think.

Because this is a sad thing, and always will be.

Today, everything is perfectly fine. The people closest to me are still alive, I am still doing work I love, and I am still healthy, or at least unaware of any serious diseases lurking inside of me.

My first husband is still dead, and always will be. That hurts today, and will hurt when you read these words, but what that pain will feel like months from now? I cannot say.

Last week I officiated a funeral for a man I had never met. He was a friend of a friend, and his wife got in touch with me and I said, yes, of course I would come be the nondenominational internet-ordained clergy for a complete and total stranger.

The front row was, of course, for the widow and her children, the people closest to this beloved man. In rows and rows behind them sat his many friends, colleagues, and family members, each holding their own personal grief for this same man, each in seats I'd been in before. Sometimes we're the widow, and sometimes we're the old co-worker standing in the back, wondering why we're crying so hard for a person who only ever passed us a few times a week in the hallways, offering a friendly hello.

When the service was over, I drove home and cried for this man I had never met. He was a person whose loss blew a huge hole in the center of several lives, and left indelible marks on many others, and didn't even touch mine. Yet we were all in that same room, and we are all in the same room. Someday, those people in the very back will find themselves in the front row at a funeral. Someday, those children in the front row will be standing in the back of another funeral parlor.

I will not tell you that every cloud has a silver lining. I'm sure that's meteorologically unsound. I can tell you that the clouds of grief shift over time. They won't always be as dark or thick as they are today. But they will never fully evaporate, either.

Instead, you'll eventually be able to see them differently, the way you'd lie on your back as a child and watch new forms emerge from those puffs of cottony vapor floating overhead. A terrible dragon would melt into a little bunny and then into a race car, a ship . . .

Whatever your clouds bring you, however they change and morph, just keep your eyes open.

ACKNOWLEDGMENTS

Everything in life is more intertwined than you can possibly imagine, like a tangle of thrift-store necklaces. This book only exists because my lovely editor Ben lost his husband and found the Hot Young Widows Club, which only exists because I met Moe Richardson, the friend I never wanted, and the one I couldn't live without. I only have her, and the Hot Young Widows Club, because of Andrew Richardson and Aaron Purmort, our dead husbands. And we only had Andy and Aaron because of every single boy we kissed, or hurt, or were hurt by.

This is a book that owes its existence to heartbreak, in all its forms. I hope it heals your bruised little ticker as much as it can.

PS—Michelle Quint of TED is a remarkably talented editor, and I thank her for taking care of this weird little book and making it better in every way.

ABOUT THE AUTHOR

Nora McInerny has a lot of jobs. She is the reluctant cofounder of the Hot Young Widows Club (a program of her nonprofit, Still Kickin), the bestselling author of the memoirs *It's Okay to Laugh (Crying Is Cool Too)*, and *No Happy Endings,* and the host of the award-winning podcast *Terrible, Thanks for Asking*. Nora is a master storyteller known for her dedication to bringing heart and levity to the difficult and uncomfortable conversations most of us try to avoid, and also for being very tall. She was voted Most Humorous by the Annunciation Catholic School Class of 1998.

Nora McInerny's TED Talk, available for free at TED.com, is the companion to *The Hot Young Widows Club.*

PHOTO: CALLIE GIOVANNA

RELATED TALKS

Andrew Solomon
How the worst moments in our lives make us who we are

Writer Andrew Solomon has spent his career telling stories of the hardships of others. Now he turns inward, bringing us into a childhood of adversity, while also spinning tales of the courageous people he's met in the years since. In a moving, heartfelt, and at times downright funny talk, Solomon gives a powerful call to action to forge meaning from our biggest struggles.

Michelle Knox
Talk about death while you're still healthy

Do you know what you want when you die? Do you know how you want to be remembered? In a candid, heartfelt talk about a subject most of us would rather not discuss, Michelle Knox asks each of us to reflect on our core values around death and share them with our loved ones, so they can make informed decisions without fear of having failed to honor our legacies. "Life would be a lot easier to live if we talked about death now," Knox says.

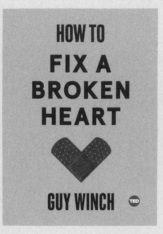

How to Fix a Broken Heart
by Guy Winch

Imagine if we treated broken hearts with
the same respect and concern we have
for broken arms. With great wisdom
and empathy, psychologist Guy Winch
explores how different our lives and our
society would be if we better understood
this unique emotional pain.

When Strangers Meet
How People You Don't Know Can
Transform You
by Kio Stark

Kio Stark invites you to discover the
unexpected pleasures and exciting
possibilities of talking to people you
don't know. Stark reveals how these
simple, surprising encounters push
us toward greater openness and
tolerance—and also how these fleeting
but powerful emotional connections can
change you, and the world we share.

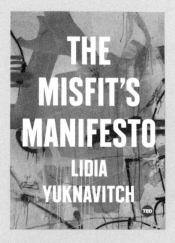

The Misfit's Manifesto
by Lidia Yuknavitch

By reclaiming and celebrating the word *misfit*, this manifesto makes a powerful case for not fitting in—for recognizing the beauty, and difficulty, in forging an original path.

In Praise of Wasting Time
by Alan Lightman

In today's frenzied and wired world, we are obsessed with the idea of not "wasting time." But have we lost the silences and solitude so essential to our inner lives?

TED is a nonprofit devoted to spreading ideas, usually in the form of short, powerful talks (eighteen minutes or less) but also through books, animation, radio programs, and events. TED began in 1984 as a conference where Technology, Entertainment, and Design converged, and today covers almost every topic—from science to business to global issues—in more than 100 languages. Meanwhile, independently run TEDx events help share ideas in communities around the world.

TED is a global community, welcoming people from every discipline and culture who seek a deeper understanding of the world. We believe passionately in the power of ideas to change attitudes, lives, and, ultimately, our future. On TED.com, we're building a clearinghouse of free knowledge from the world's most inspired thinkers—and a community of curious souls to engage with ideas and each other, both online and at TED and TEDx events around the world, all year long.

In fact, everything we do—from the TED Radio Hour to the projects sparked by the TED Prize, from the global TEDx community to the TED-Ed lesson series—is driven by this goal: How can we best spread great ideas?

TED is owned by a nonprofit, nonpartisan foundation.